Getting through it with CBT:
A young person's guide to Cognitive Behavioural Therapy (CBT)

By Dr Claire Holdaway and Dr Nicola Connolly

Series Editor: Dr Claudia Herbert

Contents

Introduction to this series   03
What is Cognitive Behavioural Therapy (CBT)?   06
Thoughts, feelings and behaviour   07
How thoughts, feelings and behaviour link up   09
What to expect from CBT   12
What is going to happen in CBT?   14
   1. Finding out about your problem   14
   2. Setting goals   14
   3. Drawing the map: Understanding your problems   15
   4. Spotting feelings   15
   5. Changing your behaviour - what am I doing?   17
   6. Catching spiky thoughts   19
   7. Looking for evidence - can I think about this
       differently?   21
   8. Weighing it up   23
   9. Testing it out   26
  10. Preparing for the future   27
Finding a therapist   28
Further information   29
Index   30
Feedback form   31

With thanks to Ben Gurney-Smith, Louise Dalton, Alice Farrington and to the young people who made comments on earlier drafts of this booklet

Introduction to this Series – 'Getting through it with CBT'

You may have been told by an adult, maybe one of your parents, a teacher, your G.P., or somebody else who you know, that getting some help for what's currently troubling you could be a good idea. Maybe you have asked for some help by yourself. You may also still just be thinking about whether it might be a good idea to find somebody who could help you with what's difficult for you at the moment. You may wonder what you could do to seek help. Also, about the kind of help that would be most useful to you.

Wherever you are in this process, understanding how therapy works and how it could help you might seem like a bit of a puzzle to you. This new series of books has been written to help you exactly with that. They talk about a specific type of therapy, which is called Cognitive Behavioural Therapy or CBT, for short. This is not the only type of therapy you could be doing that might help you with your problems. It is only one type.

CBT has been tested widely. It has been shown that for many problems it works very well. Many who have tried it, find it very helpful. This is because in CBT your therapist will actively support you to find your own solutions to some of the difficulties you currently feel stuck with. CBT involves you trying things out for yourself. That way you can discover what works best for you. You can then use these new discoveries about yourself and make changes to things that are currently a problem for you.

The first book in this series is written to help you understand how CBT works. It will give you an overview of the kinds of things that might happen in CBT therapy. This book could also be very helpful to share with a parent or teacher so that they understand more about CBT. All the other books in this series deal with specific types of problems you may be facing. For example, feeling anxious, being depressed, having obsessive compulsive behaviour, coping with loss and bereavement, coping with traumatic events, coping with bullying, and many others. All these books are written to help you understand better how these particular problems might affect you and how CBT therapy could help you with these. They are not self-help books that are designed for you to use on your own. Their aim is to support you alongside your own work in therapy. You will find in all the books, specific monitoring sheets, that might be helpful for you to use in your therapy. You should explore this with your therapist. If you have bought the books, you can download these sheets and print them from the following website: www.oxdev.co.uk

However, you may also find these books helpful while you are still considering whether you want to ask for some specific help for your problems. They could be useful for you to share with an adult, such as a parent or your G.P., who you would like to understand more about how you are feeling and what could be done about this. This would enable them to support you better with organizing the professional help that would be useful for your current problems.

We really would like these books to be helpful to you. We are therefore very interested in any comments you would like to make about them. We are especially interested in any suggestions you have for what we could improve and do better in these books. If you would like to give us feedback about any of the books you have used, you can do this on a special feedback form at the back of each book or on our website: www.oxdev.co.uk. We will take your feedback very seriously and your confidentiality will be ensured. We will consider your views for any future editions.

We wish you much success in mastering the various steps that will help you to get through your problems.

With kind regards,

Dr Claudia Herbert
Series Editor

What is Cognitive Behavioural Therapy (CBT)?

Cognitive Behavioural Therapy sounds like quite a mouthful. It is often called CBT for short. Let us break it down.

"**Cognitive**" means how you **think** about things.

"**Behavioural**" means the things you **do** (e.g. shouting, eating, phoning friends)

"**Therapy**" is about working on your problems with a trained person who has experience in helping people with similar difficulties as you.

CBT is based on the idea that changing the way you **think** about things, can change how you **feel** and what you **do**.

CBT can help with all kinds of problems including;
- Feeling sad or depressed
- Feeling worried
- Feeling angry
- Feeling bad about yourself
- Difficulties eating
- Difficulty going to school

Thoughts, feelings and behaviour

Before we go any further it is important to let you know what we mean by "**thoughts**" "**feelings**" and "**behaviours**".

Thoughts

Thoughts are words that pop into your head throughout the day. They include comments about other people ("they're really annoying") or comments about yourself ("I'm useless").

Thoughts are not always facts. They are the way we see the world.

"Man. United are the best"
"I'm stupid"
"I fancy you"
"Everyone is laughing at me"
"I can't do this"
"I love chips"
Other thoughts…

"I love chips"

"Man. United are the best"

"I'm stupid"

"I can't do this"

eryone is laughing at me"

07

Feelings

We all experience lots of different feelings

Sad

Happy

Excited

Worried

Angry

Confident

Other feelings

Body reactions

Different feelings can show in the way our body feels

Tense muscles

Sweaty

Heart racing

Relaxed

Fast breathing

Full of energy

Sick

Shaky

Other body reactions

Things we do (behaviour)

Running away

Finishing work

Crying

Going shopping

Not speaking to family or friends

Listening to music

Other behaviours

How thoughts, feelings and behaviours link up

We've been talking about how our thoughts, feelings and behaviours are all connected, but what exactly do we mean by that?

Let's use an example to try and explain.

John and Tina are brother and sister. Every morning they dash to get to the school bus which leaves at 8:15am exactly (the bus driver is a bit grumpy and doesn't wait around for very long!).

One day, John ran out of the house and down the path, where he skidded on some dog mess (kindly left by their next-door neighbour's dog, Fifi).

John **thought** to himself: *"I'm so stupid. Everyone will laugh at me in school. My whole day is ruined!"*

He **felt** so upset by this that he went home and he didn't even go to football practice that evening either (**behaviour**).

Tina came out of the house 10 minutes later and ran down the path. Just like John, she too skidded on the dog poo.

Tina **thought** *"thank goodness I've remembered to wear my shoes today!"* She laughed and shrugged her shoulders and went off to school (**behaviour**), feeling happy.

You can see from this example that, although both Tina and John step in the dog mess, how they **feel** and what they **do** depends upon how they **THINK** about the situation.

It can be helpful to think of thoughts, feelings and behaviour linking up in a cycle like the one shown below.

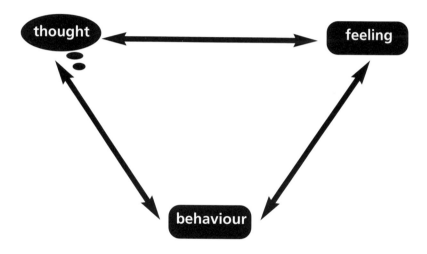

Spiky thoughts

Some thoughts, like Tina's, make us feel good, we call these **Smooth thoughts**. Other unhelpful thoughts, like John's, can make us feel sad, angry or worried. We call these **Spiky thoughts** (because they hurt us). Once spiky thoughts get a grip, they can stop us from getting on with our lives. We can feel like we're in a spiral that keeps taking us down.

Spiky thoughts can be difficult to notice. They pop into your head and are gone in a couple of seconds. Spiky thoughts can appear as words (like an annoying song that gets played over and over again), or as pictures in your mind. Sometimes you might get both at the same time. CBT helps you practice catching those thoughts that get you down, and helps you think about them differently. This can stop them whizzing around in your mind.

What to expect from CBT

One of the most important things about CBT is that the therapist is not a teacher who is there to lecture you, (yawn yawn), nor are they an expert who has the answer to all your problems. He/she is someone with special ideas and skills, who can help you to think differently about things and help you to make the changes you want to make in your life.

CBT is not about your therapist doing all the work, it is not about you doing all the work, it is about you working together.

What CBT doesn't do

It is not a magic wand, so you won't feel instantly better. It is going to take time and effort to challenge those spiky thoughts.

CBT is not just about "thinking positively" or "pulling yourself together". It is about:
- learning skills to fight back against the spiky thoughts
- learning new ways to handle your feelings
- trying out new behaviours

What is going to happen in CBT?

Listed below are the steps that you are likely to work through in your therapy.

1. Finding out about your problems
2. Setting goals
3. Drawing the map: Understanding your problems
4. Spotting feelings
5. Changing your behaviour - What am I doing?
6. Catching spiky thoughts
7. Looking for evidence - Can I think about this differently?
8. Weighing it up
9. Testing it out
10. Preparing for the future

1. Finding out about your problems

Before you can start to change things in your life, you need to figure out what isn't working - the problems.

Spiky thoughts! Spiky thoughts!... Sometimes it is hard to see what the problems are. You may feel you have so many you don't know where to start. You and your therapist will spend time thinking about what your problems are. You will learn to break down big impossible problems, into smaller pieces, which feel easier to tackle.

2. Setting goals

Once you have worked out what your problems are, you and your therapist will think about how you want things to be different. This is called goal setting. By the end of this, you will have a list of goals that you can work towards. Remember, these are your goals, not your therapist's and not your parents'.

3. Drawing the map: Understanding your problems

Understanding how your thoughts, feelings and behaviours link together helps you work out what things you need to change to reach your goals.

You and your therapist will spend time looking at your thoughts, feelings and behaviours, using them to help you draw a map of your problems. This won't help you find your way through the Amazon Jungle, but it should give you clues about what things are **making** you feel bad and what things are **keeping** you feeling bad.

Once you've got your map, its time to go away and start spotting the thoughts, feelings and behaviours that get you into sticky situations.

Hang on! Not too fast! That's a lot to do at once. Lots of people get confused between thoughts and feelings so you might need to practice spotting the difference.

4. Spotting feelings

Lots of people find it hard to understand feelings and may need help to recognise them. These are some ideas that might help.

- Talking about feelings. This is a good way of trying to untangle all the different feelings we have. Sometimes we get stuck finding a word that describes how we feel. You and your therapist might find new words to describe your feelings, or you may use pictures or models.

- Listening to our body. Different feelings make our body feel different. If we can learn to listen to our body it can help us work out what we're feeling. For example, if our body is relaxed, it might tell us that we're feeling quite calm. If our muscles are tense or we have a pain in our stomach, it might mean that we are feeling worried.

- Writing about feelings can be helpful as it allows you to think about;
  - How you let others know what you are feeling
  - What helps you feel better
  - What makes you feel worse

Tip. Writing feelings down in a feelings diary helps you start noticing and understanding your feelings, and how they are linked to what is happening around you.

Situation (what was I doing?)	Feeling	Physical feeling (what did this feel like in my body?)	Behaviour (what I did)
Made a mistake in school	Worried	Sick Tense Headache	Didn't go to school the next day

Once you have learnt to notice and understand your feelings, the next step may be to think about different ways of coping with them.

5. Changing your behaviour - What am I doing?

Learning new skills, or finding ones that you've forgotten you have, is all part of looking at your behaviour.

Remember your map. You and your therapist will spend time working out which behaviours make your problems worse and which make them better. Once you have worked this out, you and your therapist will choose which behaviours you can change first.

Tip. It's usually best to change the easiest behaviours first and work up to the really difficult ones.

For example

When Jane felt depressed and her friends asked her to go out, she used to say "no". This kept Jane feeling depressed as it made her think life was boring and sad. After a while, Jane's friends stopped asking her to go out and Jane began to think no-one liked her. These spiky thoughts made Jane feel even more depressed.

Jane's unhelpful behaviour was "**not going out**". Jane decided to try to change her behaviour and go out more. Jane found that she enjoyed being out, her friends started asking her out again and she began to feel less depressed.

Behaviours which may be keeping your problem going include:

- Avoiding people or situations
- Stopping doing things you used to enjoy
- Always having to do things in a certain way

Jane found changing her behaviour helped improve her mood and gave her a chance to try out new ways of behaving.

When Sunita felt angry she always used to shout at her mum. Her mum shouted back and then Sunita felt even more cross. This used to end up with Sunita being grounded.

Sunita and her therapist thought about different things (**skills**) she could do when she felt angry. These included;

- Listening to her favourite music to chill out
- Kicking a ball around the garden
- Holding her breath and counting to 10
- Trying to talk to her mum

The next time Sunita felt angry, instead of shouting, she tried out some of her new skills. Sunita found that this helped her feel more in control of her anger, rather than letting it control her.

6. Catching spiky thoughts

Now we have looked at feelings and behaviour, we move on to catching **Spiky thoughts**.

Spiky thoughts often tell you bad things about yourself, other people and the future. These are the thoughts that keep your problems going, a bit like the wood on a fire, which keeps it burning.

Usually we don't stop to think about our thoughts, so this bit can be quite tricky to learn.

"Hanna wants to use me"

There are a few helpful steps, which will help you start to catch your spiky thoughts:

1. You will need to get used to listening to your thoughts

2. Noticing a sudden change in how you are feeling can be a good clue that you have just had a spiky thought

3. Once you can catch your thoughts, you need to notice which ones are spiky and which ones are smooth. Remember it's the spiky ones that keep the problem going

"Tomorrow is a bad day"

"I am too fat"

To help you get even better at catching spiky thoughts you need to spot:

A. WHEN THE THOUGHTS COME
Smooth thought:
When I am playing football with my mates in the park I think "I am good at football."

Spiky thought:
When I have to play football in PE lessons I think "I am rubbish at football."

B. HOW THE THOUGHTS MAKE YOU FEEL
Smooth thought:
When I think "I am good at football." I feel happy.

happy

Spiky thought:
When I think "I am rubbish at football." I feel sad.

sad

C. WHAT THE THOUGHTS MAKE YOU DO
Smooth thought:
When I think "I am good at football." I feel happy and I score a goal.

Spiky thought:
When I think "I am rubbish at football." I feel sad and say I feel sick and can't play.

These questions may help you catch the spiky thoughts:

- What was going through my mind just before I began to feel this way?
- What does this say about me, my life, my future?
- What am I afraid might happen?
- What does this mean about how the other person might feel about me?
- What does this situation say to me about other people in general?

Tip. Try to trap your thoughts and feelings onto paper as soon as they happen. This isn't always possible, so you may need to remember them and write them down as soon as you can.

7. Looking for evidence: Can I think about this differently?

Once you have learnt to catch spiky thoughts you can check out if they are true or not. Remember, thoughts are not facts, but spiky thoughts can boss you into thinking that they are true.

We often believe all our thoughts. We think: "It is true because I thought it". But if you thought the grass was pink would that mean it was true?

After you have caught the spiky thought the next step is to question it carefully. You may find there is a different way of looking at the situation which can change the way you feel. To do this we need to find out what evidence there is to support the spiky thought and what evidence there is against it. This evidence will help you question your thought, is it really as spiky as you thought it was?

Some people can find this a bit strange and confusing at first, so to help you get used to this, there are a number of steps which you can take.

1. Start by writing down the reasons (evidence for) which you think support the spiky thought.

2. Get together the reasons (evidence against) against the spiky thought being true all of the time. This might seem difficult at first, but the following questions can help you:

The 'best mate' question:
How would someone else I respect think about this situation? What would they say to make me feel better?

The 'last time' question:
What actually happened the last time I was in this situation?

The 'is it so bad' question:
What if it does happen, what would be so bad about that?

The 'what could I do' question:
What could I actually do to deal with the situation?

The 'hard time' question:
Am I giving myself a hard time?

The 'time travel' question:
If I travelled in time three years ahead, how would I look at it?

The 'tunnel vision' question:
Am I forgetting what I can do to deal with the situation?

8. Weighing it up

After you have collected all the evidence it is time to weigh up the evidence for and against the spiky thought. Is there another way you can think about the situation?

When we first get a spiky thought we often think we have lots of evidence supporting it. "Of course it's true". However, when we weigh it up, we may find that there is more evidence against the spiky thought, than there is for it. "Maybe it's not so true". Once we have done this we can work on finding a smooth thought. We can use this next time the spiky thought comes along.

Tip. The best way to learn how to do this, is to practice writing down the evidence for and the evidence against the spiky thought. It is also helpful to write your argument against the spiky thought down, this can help you question it next time it tries to bother you.

Let's practice by looking at Jake's example:

When Jake made a mistake in school, he often got a spiky thought *"I'm going to get into terrible trouble"*. This made him feel worried and sick. Jake stayed at home and didn't go to school when he felt like this.

Jake wanted to see if there was a different way he could think about what happened. He wrote down his spiky thought and thought about the evidence for and against it.

diary can be downloaded from www.oxdev.co.uk

20/06/2004

Situation	Feeling	Spiky thought	Evidence for	Evidence against	Weighing it all up
Went to Head of Year when hadn't done homework	Worried	I'll be in terrible trouble	Teacher shouted at me once	Head of Year wasn't cross, asked how teachers could help me understand. Remember worrying about geography project. Teacher had said it was good. When Ali blamed me for smashing window, teacher listened and believed me.	I've never been in terrible trouble before. I try my best and if I make a mistake it's not the end of the world. Everyone makes some mistakes.

Looking at Jake's diary you can see that he found more evidence against the thought than there was to support it, so it couldn't always be true.

Weighing it all up, Jake decided that there was another way of thinking about what had happened. He wrote this in his diary.

When Jake tried out his new thought he found that he felt much less worried and he no longer felt sick. This new thought helped Jake stay in school rather than go home every time he felt worried.

Catching the spiky thought and questioning it was hard at first, as it was good at sneaking in and making Jake feel worried. However, the more he practised the better he got, and the better he got, the less the spiky thought came.

Sometimes people think in pictures and these pictures make them feel sad, angry, worried etc. You and your therapist may talk about the kinds of pictures you get and how you could change them to stop you feeling so bad. Sometimes it can be easier to do this than to tell someone in words, how you are feeling or what you are thinking.

9. Testing it out

If your belief in the spiky thought does not reduce, it may be because you have got so used to the spiky thought that you have not had the chance to gather evidence against it.

The best way to tackle stubborn spiky thoughts is to test them out for yourself to see what actually happens. "Testing it out", is about changing the things we do, or trying out new things, that will help us gather more evidence against the spiky thought.

Let's think about Jake again. Rather than just agreeing with his spiky thought, to find out what would happen if he made a mistake he:

- Decided to practice going to lessons he thought he might get into trouble in
- Handed in a piece of maths work he thought wasn't good enough

Jake found that the teacher didn't say anything to Jake when he went to her lesson, whilst his maths teacher congratulated Jake on handing in his work.

This helped Jake gather more evidence against the spiky thought, "I'll get into trouble".

10. Preparing for the future

Sometimes people find that after things start getting better, they have a bad patch where it feels like they are right back where they started. At these times it is really important to remember that you have learnt skills that helped you get through your problems before, so you will be able to do it again.

At the end of therapy, you and your therapist will probably spend time thinking about the things that you have found most helpful and will work on a plan for you to use in the future.

Once you have learnt CBT skills, they do need to be practiced on a regular basis so you can keep doing them well. You might be surprised how the things you've learnt can help you out in lots of different situations in the future.

Finding a therapist

Your General Practitioner (GP) should direct you towards local services where therapy is available free, as part of the NHS. There are also organisations that offer CBT on a private basis, in which case therapy would need to be paid for. If you are seeing a therapist, you have the right to ask about your therapist's qualifications, change therapists if you are unhappy and to check that your therapist is registered with a professional organisation, such as the British Psychological Society (BPS).

With CBT, the overall monitoring and accreditation organisation is the British Association of Behavioural and Cognitive Psychotherapies (BABCP). The address for the BABCP is:
  BABCP
  PO Box 9
  Accrington
  BB5 0XB

  info@babcp.com
  Tel 01254 875277

Further Information

www.youngminds.org.uk
An organisation for young people, their parents and
professionals concerned about young people's mental health

www.bullying.co.uk
For people who have been bullied

www.childline.org.uk
For children in trouble or danger
Tel: 0800 1111

www.mindbodysoul.gov.uk
Information for young people about mental health

www.rethink.org/at-ease
For young people who are under stress or worried about their
thoughts and feelings

Parents' Information Service
0800 0182138

Samaritans
08457 909090
jo@samaritans.org

Index

Behaviour 06,08
    changing your behaviour 17
    definition 06
Behavioural experiments see testing it out 26
Body reactions 08
Cognitive Behavioural Therapy (CBT) how thoughts, feelings & behaviours link up 09, 10
    what to expect from CBT 12
Feelings 08
    definition 08
    spotting feelings 15,16
Finding a therapist 28
Further information 29
Goals 14
Preparing for the future 27
Problem 14,15
    definition 14,15
Sort your thoughts 07, 11, 19
Testing it out 26
Thoughts 07
    catching spiky thoughts 19
    definition 07
    looking for evidence 21
    smooth thoughts 20
    spiky thoughts 11, 19
    testing it out 26
    weighing it up 23
Understanding your problems 12,14
Websites 16, 24, 28, 29, 32

Can you help us please?

This is a short questionnaire to help us find out what kind of people read this book, and more importantly, which parts were helpful and which were not so helpful.

Please answer the questions as best you can and return the form to: Blue Stallion Publications, 8a Market Square, Witney, OX28 6BB by post, or complete the online questionnaire at: www.oxdev.co.uk

We assure you that we will deal strictly confidentially with all given information. That means that we would never release any personal information to a third party. We will only use the information to evaluate and improve the books.

How old are you? ☐ years
Are you male or female?   Male ☐   Female ☐
Who do you live with?   Mum ☐   Dad ☐
   Brothers, how many ☐
   Sisters, how many ☐
   Grandparents ☐
   Other ☐

What made you read the book?

Who recommended this book to you?

Who did you read it with?
By yourself ☐
With a parent(s) ☐
With a doctor/therapist ☐
With someone else ☐

Have you ever been to see a therapist/psychologist to help with your
difficulties?   Yes ☐   No   ☐

Did the book make therapy any easier for you?
                                Yes ☐   No   ☐
                  No difference ☐

How helpful have you found this book?
Please mark on the scale below.

1	**2**	**3**	**4**	**5**
Not at all helpful	Not that helpful	Quite helpful	Very helpful	Extremely Helpful

Did you find it easy to understand?

1	**2**	**3**	**4**	**5**
Extremely easy to understand	Mostly easy to under-stand	Some easy parts, some difficult to understand	Quite difficult to understand	Very difficul to understand

What was the most helpful thing you learned from this book?

Was there anything you didn't like about the book?

Would you recommend this book to someone else who had
difficulties?   Yes ☐   No   ☐

Please add anything else that you think might be helpful for us to know.

Thank you for your information!

The Publisher